Healing Crystals

Healing Crystals

The Beginner's Guide to Healing Crystals and Their Meanings and Uses

Includes Types of Healing Crystals and Their Uses and How to Clean, Clear, Charge, and Activate Your Crystals

Shawna Blood

If you enjoy this book and find it helpful in learning about Crystals, I would be forever grateful if you could leave a review on Amazon. Reviews are the best way to help your fellow Crystal healers find the helpful books.

In fact, as a special gift to my fellow Crystal healers and as a thank you for buying my book, I want to send you a body boost crystal absolutely FREE! Since you've purchased the paperback version, you can also get the Kindle version for free which has the link to get your free body boost crystal.

Copyright © 2018 by Shawna Blood

All rights reserved. No part of this publication may be reproduced, distributed, or transmitted in any form or by any means, including photocopying, recording, or other electronic or mechanical methods, without the prior written permission of the publisher, except in the case of brief quotations embodied in critical reviews and certain other noncommercial uses permitted by copyright law.

CAC Publishing
ISBN: 978-1-948489-08-9
Shawna Blood

Table of Contents

Chapter 1 – Introduction to Crystals 8
    The Power of Crystals 8
Chapter 2 - Types of Crystals and Their Uses 12
Chapter 3 – Common Conditions and Healing Crystals 54
Chapter 4 - Clean and Clear your Crystals 88
    Cleansing with Water 88
    Clearing your Crystal 91
    Other Sources to Clear Your Crystals 94
Chapter 5 - Charging your Crystals 96
    Infusing It with Your Own Energy 100
Chapter 6 - Activating Your Crystal 101
Chapter 7 - Final Thoughts 102

Chapter 1 – Introduction to Crystals

Crystals are a solid layer of minerals. They can form from the lava of volcanoes and many other solutions. When liquid rock cools, or from evaporation, or from pressure. This process is called crystallization. Only crystals that have no interference or mixing of different minerals will grow large. Not to be confused with rocks. Rocks can contain many different minerals, while crystals are a purely formed single mineral. Even the simple evaporation of ocean water will lead to crystals. These are the crystals we know as salt.

Certain minerals are quite plentiful while others are quite rare. The rarer a mineral the more valuable a crystal formed from it will be.

The Power of Crystals

Crystals have been revered for their healing and protective properties since ancient times.

Archeologists have unearthed proof that the earliest of men used crystals, possibly for their spiritual or healing properties. It is because of the crystals atomic make up, along with its mineral composition, that it creates an electromagnetic force which is believed to give the crystal healing properties of a spiritual and physical nature.

Crystals are created by earth and nature, both of which have a strong connection to spirituality in several belief systems.

The electromagnetic properties of a crystal will vary, and is dependent on its color, shape, mineral composition, and its own individual atomic movement. It's thickness, the amount of light that can pass through it or be displaced by it, will also play a role in its healing abilities.

There is some documented proof that the earliest of man used crystals in a multitude of ways. They were worn during rituals, crushed into powders and made into medicines for healing, and carried as part of ceremonies.

The knowledge of which crystals are best suited for which healing purposes has been passed down for centuries. Couple that with the increasing interest in natural healing and it has made them quite popular to this day.

Crystals can be obtained in three different forms. One popular form is polished and set in jewelry of some sort, or just polished smooth and left on their own. They can be worn or carried in a pocket, or sewn into clothing. They are touched or stroked during meditation or rituals for healing.

Another form is the rough, unpolished crystal left totally in its natural state after having been mined from rocks. It is thought that rough crystals in their natural state contain the strongest power. Regardless of their form, all crystals are made up of tiny atoms in constant motion which creates energy. Just as people are affected by their actions and their environment, so are the crystals we choose. The crystals both take in and emit energy and are affected by those who use them. When you touch a crystal, it is affected by you, by your state of mind and mood, just as you are affected by the energy the crystal emits. Crystals are also affected by light and color. Both the light they absorb and the light that passes through them.

The color of a crystal will have an effect on the energy of a human, which can cause a change to that energy. When used correctly, this can bring a person into harmony with their environment. This is called Crystal therapy and is just one category of alternative medicine. Using crystals to bring oneself into balance and harmony with the spiritual and environmental factors helps to relieve stress and promote health. The theory being that many illnesses, whether mental or physical, are caused by being out of balance with one's spiritual and physical being. Using crystals can alleviate this.

Chapter 2 - Types of Crystals and Their Uses

Agate

Color

Comes in a vast array of colors.

Use

For healing the mind. This crystal is one of the oldest good luck stones. It aids in obtaining better physical and emotional balance, promotes consciousness, builds self-confidence, and offers prosperity and protection to children. Agate helps us with patience, offers awareness to any situation, fertility, avoids miscarriages and eases discomfort throughout pregnancy. Agate is also a cooling stone used for the liver, stomach, spleen, colon, and kidneys. It is also obtained for sustaining blood sugar levels, vertigo, headache and weakened balance, food problems, and lymph nodes. Wonderfully, it can help to restore nerve feeling and healing after injuries and burns.

Amethyst

Color

Deep brilliant purple to lighter shades of violet.

Use

Balancing hormones. Menopause issues, menstrual issues, fertility disorders. Amethyst is a reflective and calming stone which helps you in the expressive, divine, and physical planes to endorse peace, balance, and harmony. It is also used to remove impatience.

This stone was most vastly valued in the ancient world, and remains one of the most valued by many individuals today.

Angelite

Color

Light Blue.

Use

Brings balance to the mind, spirit and body. Angelite is used to clear energy paths. It can also be used for reprieve from throat inflammations, and to balance the thyroid. This stone also repairs and calms tissues and blood vessels. In addition, it can be extremely beneficial for weight control.

Apatite

Color

Comes in multiple shades of blue, green, reddish brown.

Use

Can aid in weight loss. Apatite also provides balance to your emotions. It is a stone of manifestation and will show you how to turn your thoughts into reality and receive the results you desire. It means service to other individuals and being involved in charitable quests. Apatite is in harmony with the future and also associated with past lives.

Aquamarine

Color

Pale blue.

Use

Used for protection, especially during travel. Helps with allergy symptoms. Promotes peace and joy. Aquamarine is said to enhance the happiness of marriages. The best way to wear this stone is in contact with your skin, particularly close to the wounded portion of the body. This stone is known to help with eye inflammation, arthritis, varicose veins, and sore throat.

Aragonite

Color

Comes in shades of red, orange or brown. Sometimes white.

Use

Helps with irritability. Used to promote hair growth and clear skin. Aragonite helps to alter moods by relieving negative emotions like anxiety and stress. It can help you feel more grounded and centered.

Aragonite can also help heal the body. It is known to help with the symptoms of Raynaud's Disease. Muscle spasms and chills are also soothed by this stone.

Aventurine

Color

Light to dark green.

Use

Use for gaining control of emotions. Helpful with heart and respiratory problems. Bring Aventurine to a job interview to raise your chances of being hired. Also, bring it with you on a date to increase the chances that the date will go well.

Aventurine will ignite creativity, imagination and provide mental focus and clarity. It is a stone of hopefulness, seeing the good in any circumstance and making a negative into a positive.

Black Obsidian

Color

Deep black, darkest brown or dark green.

Use

For protection against negative forces. Promotes stability. Black Obsidian is a stone of truth. It can divulge numerous secrets and also answer your main questions about love and life. This stone will provide the meaning of some of the biggest mysteries in your life, the folks you love, and the world overall.
Basically, it is the stone of honesty.

Black Tourmaline

Color

Solid black or streaked with gray and brown.

Use

Used to purify and protect. Good for arthritis and lower back pain. Black Tourmaline is a powerful stone used for shield against negative energy, and is a solid spiritual grounding stone. Black Tourmaline is one of the most popular crystals used for metaphysical purposes. It is by far the best protection stone that you can use. It inspires positive attitudes, happiness and good luck. This stone will be a positive force for good in your life.

Bloodstone (The Coach)

Color

Red or dark green. Sometimes black with streaks of red.

Use

Used for protection. Helps with depression and helps balance hormones. Encourages self-esteem, harmony and balance. Used as an aphrodisiac in India.
Is thought to strengthen and oxygenate the bloodstream, aiding in easing blood-related illnesses. Helpful in regulating the menstrual flow, and calming painful cramps. A general healing stone which helps to clear and cleanse the body's energy.

Chiastolite (Cross Stone)

Color

Green, red, Brown, White or Orange. Will have a cross.

Use

Used for blood pressure and circulation. This stone is used for balance and harmony. It will counter differences among individuals of opposing ideas, and convert their defiance into harmonious agreement. The Chiastolite is known to be supportive in boosting your creativity, and also has an energy that improves problem solving skills. This is an uplifting stone if you are suffering an illness. It is also known to comfort the dying as they approach spirit.

Chlorite

Color

Green, white, yellow, red, purple or black.

Use

For all aspects of healing. Chlorite helps to make you feel balanced and linked with Nature. It is calming, relaxing, soothing and peaceful. It helps you to slow down and enjoy the present moment, stabilizes emotions and moods, and eases a troubled heart.

Works for self-healing, as well as global healing. Removes negative energy including sickness, aggression and anger. Purifies your aura, lines up and rejuvenates your Chakras, bringing balance to your whole being.

Citrine

Color

Yellow and orange.

Use

Helps with digestive problems and increases mental clarity. Citrine is a remarkable crystal. It does not hold negative energy. Instead, it transforms it to positive. Therefore, it never needs to be cleared. It can also be used for healing or meditation to alter negative energy to positive. It is a powerful stone which attracts good luck and success. It stimulates mental focus and obligation to any task, and it is thought to boost the awareness and connection with your higher self. It inspires joy and laughter. It is a great stone for manifesting your wishes.

Diamond

Color

Clear brilliant white, pink, blue, yellow, brown.

Use

To bring good luck and positive influence. Increases creativity and psychic ability. Diamond is considered a leading healer for its capability to unite the mind and body. This stone is useful in cleansing and strengthening brain function, nerves and sensory organs. Great for epilepsy, strokes and to battle aging and restore energy levels. Diamonds have been used to treat constipation, and all organs concerned with eliminating waste from the body.

Dolomite

Color

White, yellow, pink, gray, brown or black.

Use

Used to treat depression. Also, to strengthen muscles nails and hair. Dolomite is a gentle stone that inspires charitable giving as well as receiving. It also inspires energetic and original thinking, impulsiveness, imagination, and manifestation. Dolomite is also used to halt energy leaks, balance and align your chakras. When strategically placed in a home with other minerals, together with the other minerals it will balance the energetic atmosphere. Predominantly good for releasing sadness, lonesomeness, tension and worry. It is also used in crystal healing to reduce the effects of PMS and the female reproductive system. It can strengthen bones, teeth, and muscles. Pink dolomite is good for insomnia.

Emerald

Color

Brilliant grass green with shades of yellow.

Use

Used to bring love, treats fertility problems and eye sight. Emerald is the stone of the heart. It represents compassion, mercy and universal love. It also signifies the brilliant things in this world and how those things are unified with love. Emerald promotes physical, mental, emotional, and spiritual balance.

This crystal increases energy levels in your body and enhances the energy stream between the lower and upper chakras.

Flourite

Color

Purple blue, green, yellow, colorless, brown, pink, black or orange.

Use

Attracts positive energy and creates well-being. Fluorite is an extremely protecting crystal. It actually helps you know when there are outside forces attempting to manipulate you. It is predominantly useful to have at work when you are surrounded by antagonistic or conflicting forces, as it will ward off negative energies. Fluorite will cleanse your body and remove anything that may be causing it not to function correctly.

Geode

Color

White, clear, purple, blue, gray. They must be cracked open to view the color.

Use

Brings mental clarity and aids in decision making. Helps with memory. Bigger geodes can produce a chi flow in your home. Geodes can aid in communicating with celestial beings and helps you to create a better mood and be more balanced. Use Geodes when meditating, asking for relief from stress and help with decision making. Across the board, Geodes promote well-being and have numerous health benefits.

Garnet

Color

All shades of red.

Use

Increases good health and reduces negativity. Treats circulation and exhaustion. Decreases inflammation.
One of the most noteworthy characteristics of the garnet is its capability of healing and purifying. It gets rid of the toxins in your body and restores it to its re-energized state. This crystal will cleanse your body, mind, and soul. This is a must-have stone if you want to attain or reclaim your balance, feel safe and protected, and harness your inner strength.

Galena

Color

Silver, black, or gray.

Use

Brings balance and harmony. Galena can be used in past life regression to assist with inner vision. This crystal aids in confronting and overpowering your deep-rooted fears. Galena brings strength, valor and capability to face tough times.

Howlite

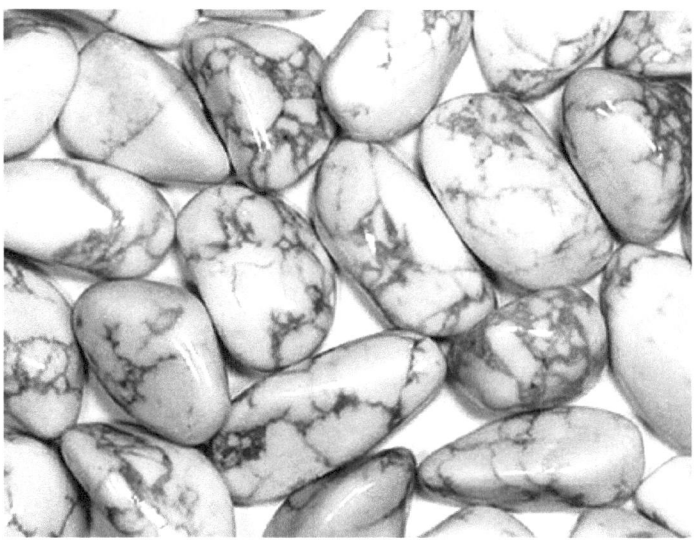

Color

White with black or gray streaks.

Use

To bring a sense of calm, reduces pain. It will provide you with knowledge and insight. Howlite will assist you in connecting to a higher realm and will eliminate the masks that are hindering the truths in your life. It is a great tool to use while meditating due to the fact that it can give you focus. Howlite endorses tranquility of mind and removes distracting thoughts. Can help you to rid you of stress and anxiety. It is a powerful and calming stone.

Hyalite Opal

Color

White, clear.

Use

To bring peace. Increase imagination and balance hormones. Hyalite is a colorless opal with a strong shine. It is wonderful for scrying. Its possesses a connection with the spirit realm. Hyalite Opal is a mood stabilizer with links the base chakra with the crown chakra. What it will do is boost the meditative experience. Hyalite assists in transitioning out of the body, as the body is only a brief vessel for the soul.

Iolite

Color

Shades of blue or purple.

Use

To strengthen intuition. Iolite will provide balance to your life. It can also be an exceptional aid for relationship problems, whether they are with friends, co-workers, parent-child, love, etc. By carrying or wearing this stone, it will help you to be more sympathetic to the plight of others. Physically, it can assist in easing the pain of headaches, migraines and eye strain. Relieves insomnia and nightmares when placed under your pillow.

Indiocolite

Color

Deep blue tourmaline.

Use

Helps with communication skills and overcoming shyness. Indiocolite is a commanding third eye chakra crystal and a powerful throat chakra stone that helps to improve communication. This will help in speaking to those in spirit.

Jasper

Color

Brownish red, yellow, white, gray or black.

Use

A healing crystal that works towards general health, overcoming shyness and for protection. Jasper is a nurturing stone. It will sustain you throughout times of stress, bring you serenity, joy, and completeness, boost your confidence, and rid you of irrational fears.
Beneficial for individuals who are experiencing burnout at work or from something personal.
Helps to achieve a healthy balance in life.

Kyanite

Color

Usually blue, can also be colorless, white, green, gray or black.

Use

Helps with communication, focuses energy, encourages tranquility, strengthens immune system. Kyanite is a stone with high vibrations and strong energy. May help with the ability to remember dreams and provides healing dreams. Works inside the third eye chakra, and is perfect to use at the throat chakra, generating improved communication and expressiveness. Helps you to speak your truth.

Labradorite

Color

Silvery gray with streaks of blue, pink, green or yellow.

Use

Helps cure gout, good for reducing cold symptoms. Labradorite can boost the connection amongst your bodily and spiritual self. It is a very spiritual crystal that helps you to move much easier into the higher realms of being between the spirit world and your standard world. This stone will boost your capabilities inside the chakras above the heart chakra.

Lapis Lazuli

Color

Blue, sometimes with white specks.

Use

General healing and helps with Insomnia. Lapis Lazuli is the best manifestation and/or meditation stone. It empowers your thoughts and protects you from psychic and physical attacks. This crystal is a good protection stone. It can help you make your dreams become reality.

Lepidolite

Color

Purple, pink, yellow, green and white.

Use

Encourages acceptance. Helps prevent nightmares. Good for general aches and pains. Lepidolite provides a soothing energy that so many individuals can profit from. The rapid pace of life is stressful enough, and there is really nothing better than a classic, soothing stone.

Malachite

Color

Shades of light to dark green.

Use

Increases psychic abilities. Helps let go of emotional baggage. Malachite intensifies all kinds of energies - positive and negative. This is one of the most significant healing stones. It helps to recognize, draw out, and release negative energy, as well as deep-rooted emotional patterns, previous traumas, and repressed emotions. Assists in learning energy blocks that might be triggering physical disease.

Moonstone

Color

Translucent with a pink blush or blue or yellow sheen.

Use

Helps balance emotions, protects against psychic attacks, reduces pain and helps with fertility issues. Moonstone helps calm stress and avoid overreaction. It provides hopefulness, improves feminine energy, understanding, insight, and psychic capabilities. Provides abundance and protection, particularly during labor, pregnancy, and travel. It is also connected with love of all kinds.

Obsidian

Color

Black with gray and white.

Use

Used for protection from negativity. Relieves pain, good for poor circulation of the extremities. The Obsidian stone is excellent to help you in your past life healing journey, specifically healing your family ancestry. Its energy will help you to deal with problems related to previous mismanagement of power.

Opals

Color

White, blue, pink, green, orange, red.

Use

Increases imagination, intuition, and psychic ability. Opal will stimulate uniqueness and increase creativity. The energy of the Opal stone will also inspire you to express your exact self. You will feel self-confident and happy in your own skin. This will exude in your words, feelings, and actions.

Peacock Ore

Color

Brown, black red, copper.

Use

Protects from negativity. Helps with metabolism, good for depression. Peacock Ore brings cheerfulness and joy. It will take you in a more positive direction and help to provide happiness to others. It provides you with the skill to realize and appreciate the enjoyment existing in every second.

Peridot

Color

Shades of green.

Use

Reduces emotional stress. Good for depression, brings luck and used for protection and weight loss. Peridot will create an improvement in your health and spirituality. The energy also helps to generate a growth of joy and love in your life. It is powerful enough to manifest a rise in the flow of money. In other words, this stone is very effective to manifest abundance and prosperity.

Rose Quartz

Color

Translucent pink.

Use

Helps in finding true love, balances emotions and heals heartache. Also thought to reduce wrinkles. Rose quartz provides solid vibrations of love, joy, warmth and emotional health. It holds energies connected to the heart chakra. Rose Quartz can provide help in finding your true love. It can open up your chakras to recognize either the best in people or signs that you should stay away from them.

Ruby

Color

Pink and red.

Use

Considered the stone of kings and royalty. Brings love, increases passion, helps with fertility, reduces fever. Ruby recharges your energy levels and stimulates your mind to be more positive and self-confident. It is very effective for inspiring liveliness, sensuality and sensual energy. Ruby is a stone of manifestation and can provide wealth of all types.

Sapphire

Color

Deep dark blue to nearly black. More rarely comes in shades of purple, red, pink, and yellow.

Use

Helps in healing all parts of the body. Increases strength. Sapphire is used generally for protection purposes. The shielding properties of this stone are extremely beneficial if you are worried about bodily, emotional, psychological, or spiritual attacks. Will provide integrity, truth, and purity.

Tiger's Eye

Color

Shades of brown and gold.

Use

Used for protection, increases courage, and willpower. Brings strength. Strengthens bones. Tiger's Eye is used to treat depression and bipolar disease. It is a perfect stone if you are seeking balance and harmony in life. Tiger's Eye can reestablish the equilibrium in your life. It is also good to release fears and anxieties, and it will provide courage, strength of mind, and self-assurance, allowing you to confront anything that comes your way.

Topaz

Color

Usually blue, more rarely yellow, brown, green rainbow, red, clear, or pink.

Use

Increases creativity, brings about mental clarity. Good for depression and gall bladder problems. Topaz is a crystal which provides love and good fortune. It is very effective for conveying fruitful achievement of goals. Will attract the right person into your life, whether it be friendship, love, business, or to simply to improve current relationships.

Tourmaline

Color

Various colors.

Use

Cleanses the aura, offers protection, brings peace, replaces negativity, attracts prosperity and intelligence. Good for arthritis pain. Tourmaline is helpful in assisting with adrenal exhaustion. Also, it holds a beneficial energy that relieves stress.

Chapter 3 – Common Conditions and Healing Crystals

Affluence
Citrine

Alienation
Garnet

Assets/Riches
Bloodstone, Citrine, Diamond, Epidote, Garnet, Jade, Malachite, Moonstone, Peridot, Topaz, Smoky Quartz, Rutilated Quartz, Tree Agate, Tsavorite, Turquoise

Melodrama
Carnelian

Heartburn
Aquamarine, Bloodstone, Garnet, Kunzite, Malachite, Turquoise, Zoisite

Obsessive Behaviors and Addictions
Agate, Amethyst Ametrine, Astrophyllite, Agate, Coral, Citrine, Dendritic Agate, Dravite, Dumortierite, Galena, Green Calcite, Diamond, Iolite, Malachite-Azurite, Nebula Stone, Obsidian, Peridot, Petrified Wood, Phenacite, Rose Quartz, Zircon

Concentration
Cerussite, Lepidolite, Petalite

Immune System
Quartz, Dolomite, Halite, Petoskey Stone, Petrified Wood

Allergy and Cold Symptoms
Apatite, Aventurine, Dolomite, Garnet

Anger and Irritability
Aquamarine, Aragonite, Lepidolite, Lithium Quartz, King Cobra Jasper, Kunzite, Kyanite, Magnetite, Peridot, Smoky Quartz, Sodalite, Turquoise

Aches Pain Arthritis
Abalone, Amber, Amethyst, Apatite, Azurite, Black Tourmaline, Lapis, Lodestone (Magnetite), Malachite, Petrified Wood, Quartz, Rhodonite, Ruby, Sulphur, Topaz

Anemia and Blood Issues
Bloodstone, Garnet, Hematite

Anxiety and Fear
Azurite-Malachite, Berlinite, Bloodstone, Cerussite, Covellite, Diopside, Dolomite, Plume Agate

Asthma Emphysema and Bronchitis
Amethyst, Azurite Malachite, Morganite, Obsidian, Tiger's Eye, Vanadinite

Attracting A Spouse
Carnelian, Rhodonite, Rhodocrosite

Aura
Ametrine, Citrine, Dravite, Epidote, Iolite, Labradorite, Quartz

Awareness
Howlite, Lapis Lazuli, Opal

Backaches
Calcite, Carnelian, Garnet, Lodestone, Obsidian

Emotional Disturbance
Ametrine, Bloodstone, Blue Topaz, Celestite, Chiastolite, Chrysoprase, Rhodochrosite, Rhodonite, Sodalite, Tektite, Tiger's Eye, Tourmaline

Balance
Emerald, Diamond Garnet, Quartz, Moonstone

Beauty
Diamond, Jasper, Ruby, Tiger's Eye

Bipolar Disorder
Ametrine, Bloodstone, Blue topaz, Chrysoprase, Diopside, Fluorite, Hematite, Kunzite, Larimar, Lepidolite, Lithium Quartz, Lodestone, Rhodochrosite, Sodalite, Tektite, Tiger's Eye, Tourmaline, Tree Agate, Turquoise

High Blood Pressure
Bloodstone, Blue Calcite, Chrysocolla, Sodalite

Low Blood Pressure
Bloodstone, Halite (Salt)

Blood Sugar (Low)
Aventurine, Serpentine

Circulatory System
Amber, Amethyst, Aventurine, Bloodstone, Fire Agate, Fluorite, Garnet, Hematite, Kunzite, Kyanite, Malachite, Moss Agate, Pyrite, Red Jasper, Ruby, Rutilated, Quartz, Salt, Sapphire, Tiger Iron, Topaz

Body Aches
Diopside

Excessive Body Odor
Jasper, Magnesite

Bones
Amazonite, Blue Lace Agate, Calcite, Dolomite, Fluorite, Malachite, Petrified Wood

Brain (Mental clarity)
Albite, Amber, Aragonite, Chalcopyrite, Clear Quartz, Garnet, Galenite, Hematite, Rhodizite

Broken Heart
Chrysoprase, Rhodonite, Salt

Bronchitis
Gold, Lodestone, Rutilated Quartz

Burns
Gem Silica

Calming
Abalone, amber, Amazonite, Amethyst, Angelite, Aragonite, Barite (especially desert rose type), Bloodstone, Blue Lace Agate, Blue Peru Opal, Blue Chalcedony, Calcite, Fluorite, Infinite Stone, Pearl, Larimar, Lepidolite, Lepidolite

Cancer Prevention
Azurite-Malachite, Fluorite, Gold, Hematite, Lapis, Lepidolite, Moonstone, Red Jasper, Rose Chalcedony, Sapphire, Tourmaline

Cardiovascular
Bloodstone, Hematite

Adjusting to Changes
Bloodstone, Botswana Agate, Chiastolite, Honey Calcite, Opal

Bringing Changes
Green Tourmaline, Emerald, Blue Sapphire

Channeling Spirits
Apophyllite, Blue Calcite, Copper, Meteorites, Kyanite, Quartz, Yellow Calcite

Childbirth and Pregnancy
Amazonite, Amethyst (prevent miscarriage), Ammonite, (for preventing miscarriage), Geodes, Hematite, Lepidolite, Malachite, Rose Quartz

Childhood Trauma
Black Diopside, Dioptase, Lithio-Laser crystal, Petalite, Rose Quartz, Watermelon Tourmaline

Crohn's Disease
Carnelian, Diopside, Thulite

Chronic Fatigue Syndrome
Amethyst, Aquamarine, Aragonite, Orange Calcite, Quartz, Rhodochrosite, Ruby, Zincate

Clairvoyance
Ametrine, Azurite-Malachite, Charoite, Diamond, Emerald, Green Jasper, Halite (salt), Hematite, Herkimer Diamond, Kyanite

Clarity
Amber, Danburite, Diamond, Dumortierite (Blue Quartz), Halite (Salt Crystal), Imperial Topaz, Sapphire, Peridot, Tiger's Eye

Claustrophobia
Chrysoprase

Cleansing
Amber, Bloodstone, Emerald, Garnet, Obsidian, Green Kunzite, Kyanite, Tiger's Eye

Cold Sores / Fever Blisters
Fluorite

Colic
Amazonite, Blue Lace Agate

Comfort
Agate, Rose Quartz, Jasper, Blue Kyanite, Pink and Green Kunzite Morrisonite Jasper

Commitment
Garnet

Communication
Amazonite, Apatite, Blue Lace Agate, Blue Onyx, Blue Tiger's Eye, Blue Topaz, Copper, Emerald, Kunzite, Labradorite, Quartz, Turquoise, Ulexite

Compassion
Green Jasper, Green Tourmaline, Jade, Kunzite, Moonstone, Kunzite, Rose Quartz, Red Jasper

Compatibility
Green Moss Agate

Completion of Tasks
Red Jasper

Concentration
Carnelian, Fluorite, Goethite, Jade, Lapis, Obsidian, Quartz Crystals, Malachite, Hematite, Ruby

Confidence
Diamond, Grossularite Garnet, Moonstone, Rhodizite Jade, Moonstone,
Tiger's Eye, Jade

Confusion
Bloodstone, Lodestone, Fluorite

Contentment
Red Jasper

Cooperation
Smoky Quartz

Courage
Agate, Amethyst, Aquamarine, Aventurine, Bloodstone, Blue Tiger's Eye, Carnelian, Charoite, Chevron Amethyst, Chrysoprase, Fire Agate, Garnet, Hematite, Herkimer Diamond, Red Calcite, Richterite, Ruby, Rutile, Sodalite, Smoky Quartz, Tiger's Eye, Variscite

Creativity
Agate, Aventurine, Azurite, Botswana Agate, Calcite, Carnelian, Citrine, Cobaltite, Dolomite, Garnet, Herkimer Diamonds, Obsidian, Peach Aventurine

Decision Making
Charoite, Crazy Lace Agate, Diamond, Emerald, Falcon's Eye (Blue Tiger's Eye), Fluorite, Jade, Lepidolite, Nephrite, Tiger's Eye

Denial / Avoidance
Rhodochrosite

Depression
Carnelian, Chrysoprase, Citrine, Kunzite, Lepidolite, Lapis, Blue Quartz, Gold, Jet, Smoky Quartz, Rose Quartz, Black Tourmaline Peridot, Botswana Agate, Lapis, Moonstone, Quartz, Platinum, Spinel, Topaz

Destiny
Charoite, Labradorite, Moonstone

Dexterity
Tuhualite

Detoxification
Covellite

Diabetes
Amethyst, Bloodstone, Quartz, Red Jasper, Sodalite

Diarrhea
Brecciated Jasper, Salt

Digestion
Blue Lace Agate, Citrine, Epidote, Peridot, Obsidian, Tiger's Eye, Topaz

Diplomacy
Lepidolite

Disillusionment
Dalmatian Jasper

Disorientation
Black Tourmaline, Hematite

Divination
Charoite, Hematite, Moonstone, Tiger's Eye

Domestic Bliss
Emerald

Dowsing
Brecciated Jasper

Dreams
Amethyst, Rose Quartz, Jade, Clear Quartz, Citrine, Jade, Kyanite, Labradorite, Lapis Lazuli, Lepidolite, Nebula Stone, Opal, Prehnite, Red Jasper, Marble, Pyrite, Smokey Quartz, Ruby, Tektites, Celestite, Jade, Marble, Ruby

Ears / Hearing
Amber, Celestite, Rhodonite

Eating Disorders
Jasper, Tuhualite

Eczema
Amazonite, Aventurine, Blue Lace Agate

Electrolytes
Mother of Pearl, Sea Shells

Employment /Job / Work (Find, Stabilize)
Aventurine (green), Citrine, Garnet (green), Jade, Malachite, Moonstone, Geodes, Peridot, Sapphire (black), Ruby, Siderite, Tourmaline (yellow)
Endocrine System: Alexandrite, Amber, Amethyst, Aquamarine, Bloodstone, Green Calcite, Chrysoberyl, Citrine, Howlite, Magnetite, Green Obsidian, Rhodochrosite, Sodalite

Endurance
Brecciated Jasper

Energy (Increase, High Energy)
Amber, Agate, Apophyllite,
Aragonite Bloodstone, Blue Calcite, Blue Goldstone, Carnelian, Clear Quartz, Danburite, Garnet, Green Jasper, Prehnite, Red Calcite, Red Coral, Rhodochrosite, Ruby, Rutilated Quartz, Spinel, Sulphur, Yellow Calcite

Energy Leaks
Dolomite

Enhance Emotions
Garnet, Ruby

Enhance Energy of Other Crystals
Apatite, Chrysoberyl, Dolomite Danburite, Diamond, Herkimer Diamonds, Quartz, Selenite

Envy
Agate

Epilepsy
Jet, Lapis

ESP
Peridot

Exploring the Unknown
Botswana Agate

Eyes / Eyesight
Aquamarine, Celestite, Charoite, Holey Stones (eyesight in particular), Labradorite, Opal, Rutilated Quartz, Mica

Faith
Emerald

Family Issues
Citrine, Family Clusters of Crystals

Fear (Dispel)
Ammonite, Aquamarine, Carnelian, Chrysoprase, Citrine, Orange Calcite, Red Calcite, Sagenite, Smoky Quartz, Sodalite

Feet
Onyx

Female Reproductive Health
Moonstone

Feminine Reproductive-Related Issues
Chrysoprase (Endometriosis), Lapis, Rose Quartz

Fertility
Carnelian, Chrysoprase, Garnet, Rose Quartz

Fevers
Aventurine, Diopside, Hematite, Peridot, Pyrite, Tree Agate, Tektite, Sapphire, Sodalite

Fibromyalgia Amber, Amethyst, Citrine, Clear Quartz, Emerald, Hematite, Lapis, Labradorite, Morganite, Obsidian, Rose Quartz, Ruby, Tiger's Eye

Fidelity
Jade, Opal

Finances, Stabilizing
Jet, Ruby

Finding Lost Objects, People
Peridot, Snakeskin Agate, Golden Topaz, Green Moss Agate (lost treasure or money)

Flu
Bloodstone

Fluid Retention
Aquamarine

Focus
Apatite, Fluorite

Fortune, Good
Bloodstone, Lodestone (Magnetite), Moonstone, Tree Agate

Friendship
Aventurine, Green Moss Agate

Gallbladder
Amber, Carnelian, Chalcedony, Citrine, Danburite, Jade, Red Jasper

Gambling Luck
Aventurine

Gardening & Agriculture
Herkimer Diamond, Jasper, Lepidolite

Generosity
Citrine, Dolomite

Grace
Blue Lace Agate, Rhodonite

Grief
Amethyst, Apache Tear, Aqua Aura, Bloodstone, Botswana Agate, Carnelian, Citrine, Chrysoprase, Jasper, Jet, Lapis Lazuli, Onyx, Pyrite, Rainbow Crystals, Rose Quartz, Smoky Quartz, Watermelon Tourmaline

Grounding
Agate, Apache Tears, Bloodstone, Black Onyx, Brecciated Jasper, Candle Quartz, Carnelian, Cuprite, Dalmatian Jasper, Fluorite, Garnet, Hematite, Obsidian, Salt, Smoky Quartz

Growth
Blue Lace Agate

Guilt
Copper, Rose Quartz, Ruby, Sodalite

Guidance
Amethyst, Green Onyx, Purple Obsidian

Grief
Obsidian, Apache Tears

Hair Loss
Aragonite, Chalcopyrite, Franklinite, Galena

Hallucinations
Jasper, Rhodochrosite, Coral

Happiness and Joy
Amazonite, Amethyst, Aventurine, Blue Lace Agate, Blue Quartz, Carnelian, Chrysoprase, Citrine, Diamond, Moonstone, Pyrite, Rainbow Crystals, Rose Quartz, Smokey Quartz

Harmonious Environment
Amber, Amethyst, Petrified Wood, Rose Quartz, Tiger's Eye, Multi-Colored Tourmaline, Tree Agate, Blue Sapphire

Headache
Amber, Amethyst, Angelite, Jasper, Aquamarine, Black Jade, Bloodstone, Blue Agate, Blue Aventurine, Blue Lace Agate, Charoite, Emerald, Fire Agate, Green Aventurine, Green Tourmaline, Holly Blue Chalcedony, Iolite, Jade, Jet, Lapis Lazuli, Malachite, Moss Agate, Blue Obsidian, Pearl, Phenacite (Phenakite), Purple Fluorite, Rhodochrosite, Rose Quartz, Silicon, Sodalite, Tiger's Eye, Turquoise

Heart
Amazonite, Amber, Beryl, Garnet, Hematite, Lapis Lazuli, Green Obsidian, Onyx,

Honesty
Garnet, Kyanite, Lapis Lazuli, Pearl, Ruby, Selenite, Sodalite, Tiger's Eye

Hunger Suppressant
Apatite, Muscovite

Imagination
Aventurine

Immune System
Amethyst, Aqua Aura, Black Tourmaline, Blue Lace Agate, Botswana Agate, Chrysoprase, Citrine, Emerald, Epidote, Fulgurites, Garnet, Green Millennium, Jade, Lapis Lazuli, Lepidolite, Lithium Quartz, Lodestone, Malachite, Moss Agate, Obsidian, Pearl, Picture Jasper, Quantum-Quattro Silica, Quartz, Rubellite, Rutilated Quartz, Smithsonite, Snow Quartz, Sulphur, Topaz

Incontinence
Petrified Wood

Infection
Pearl, Pyrite, Quartz

Inferiority
Chrysoprase

Infertility
Carnelian, Garnet, Grossularite, Garnet, Quartz Scepter, Rose Quartz, Shiva Lingam

Inflammation and Swelling
Pyrite

Inhibitions
Opal

Inner Awareness
Apache Tears, Rose Quartz

Inner Peace
Amethyst, Apatite, Aquamarine, Aventurine, Blue Topaz, Blue Tourmaline, Calcite, Celestite, Blue Fluorite, Hawk's Eye Diamond, Jade, Jasper, Kunzite, Lepidolite, Malachite, Opal, Rose Quartz, Selenite

Insect Bites
Moonstone

Insomnia
Amethyst, Celestite, Emerald, Hematite, Labradorite, Lapis, Lepidolite, Pink Dolomite, Smoky Quartz, Sodalite, Zircon

Intellect
Aquamarine, Agate, Amazonite, Amber, Ametrine, Apatite, Aventurine, Azurite, Bloodstone, Crocoite, Diopside, Emerald, Galena, Honey Calcite, Malachite, Obsidian, Pyrite, Rose Quartz, Sodalite, Spinel, Tektite, Topaz, Turquoise

Intestinal / Digestive
Amber, Aquamarine, Barite, Citrine, Clear Quartz, Pyrite, Jasper, Labradorite, Laguna Agate,
Moss Agate, Obsidian, Onyx, Peridot, Smokey Quartz

Irritable Bowel
Orange Calcite

Intuition
Amazonite, Amethyst, Azurite, Chrysolite, Emerald, Lapis, Onyx, Sodalite, Yellow Calcite

Inspiration
Aquamarine, Blue Kyanite, Kunzite Pink, Moonstone

Jealousy
Peridot

Joy
Aquamarine, Emerald, Sapphire

Karma and Protection
Morganite, Quartz Crystals, Charoite, Brown Tourmaline, Garnet

Kidney
Amber, Bloodstone, Green Calcite, Carnelian, Chrysoberyl, Coral, Cuprite, Jade, Jasper, Orange Calcite, Rhodochrosite, Smokey Quartz

Kindness
Azurite, Celestite, Chalcedony, Jasper, Kunzite, Morganite, Rhodochrosite, Rhodonite, Rose Quartz, Pink Tourmaline, Turquoise

Laughter
Crazy Lace Agate

Leadership/Management
Fossils, Trilobite

Legal Issues
Amethyst, Bloodstone, Garnet

Leg Cramps
Bloodstone

Life Purpose
Charoite, Garnet

Liver
Carnelian, Jasper

Loneliness
Jade, Dolomite, Pink Tourmaline

Longevity
Diamond, Fossils, Jasper, Tree Agate

Love
Amber, Rose Quartz, Diamond, Emerald Blue Kyanite, Moonstone, Opal, Pearl, Pink Coral, Pink Tourmaline

Romance
Emerald, Garnet, Ruby

Sex Drive
Garnet, Tiger's Eye, Ruby

Spiritual Love and Fidelity
Lapis

Unconditional Love
Kunzite, Rose Quartz, Pink Manganocalcite, Jade

Loyalty
Dalmatian Jasper

Luck
Agate, Aquamarine, Aventurine, Copper, Jade, Malachite, Moonstone, Obsidian, Pyrite, Snow Quartz, Smoky Quartz

Lungs
Peach Aventurine, Pyrite, Rutilated Quartz

Lupus
Bloodstone

Magic
Labradorite

Marriage
Pearl, Peridot

Mastery
Onyx

Meditation
Amethyst, Ametrine, Aqua Aura, Aquamarine, Azurite, Celestite, Chrysoprase, Clear Quartz, Blue Quartz), Flourite, Iolite, Kunzite, Kyanite, Labradorite, Lapis, Topaz, Tsavorite, Yellow Calcite, Quartz Crystal, Diamond

Memory
Blue Calcite, Carnelian, Emerald, Honey Calcite, Onyx, Pyrite, Quartz Crystals, Rhodochrosite, Spinel

Menopause
Amethyst, Moonstone, Pietersite

Mental Clarity
Amber, Aquamarine, Aventurine, Blue Quartz, Citrine, Quartz, Diamond Sodalite, Tiger's Eye, Topaz

Migraine
Amethyst, Green Aventurine, Purple Fluorite, Rose Quartz

Mood Swings
Citrine, Lepidolite

Muscle Pain and Healing
Abalone, Amazonite, Apatite, Emerald

Muscle and Menstrual Cramps
Amazonite, Bloodstone

Money and Business Luck
Malachite, Green Aventurine, Citrine, Gold, Ruby

Mother Earth
Turquoise, Rose Quartz, Lapis Lazuli

Nail Problems
Apatite

Narrow Mindedness
Epidote

Negativity
Carnelian, Citrine, Jade, Malachite, Obsidian, Rutilated Quartz, Salt, Selenite Black Tourmaline, Black Obsidian, Quartz

Nervous System
Alexandrite, Amazonite, Aquamarine, Apatite, Botswana Agate, Fire Agate, Emerald, Galena, Lapis Lazuli, Morganite, Peridot, Tourmaline

Nervousness
Watermelon Tourmaline

New Beginnings
Chrysoprase, Moonstone

Nightmare Prevention
Chrysoprase, Citrine, Jasper

Obsessive Compulsive Disorder
Amethyst, Chrysoprase

Old Hurts
Rhodonite

Organization
Bloodstone, Jasper, Blue Quartz, Fluorite, Green Kunzite, King Cobra Jasper, Lepidolite, Obsidian

Osteoporosis
Amazonite, Howlite

Pain Relief
Amber, Amethyst, Dolomite, Calcite, Hematite, Howlite, Infinite Stone, Lapis

Pancreas
Carnelian, Moonstone, Tiger's Eye

Panic Attacks
Epidote, Lepidolite

Paralysis
Petrified Wood

Parkinson's Disease
Opal

Passion
Emerald, Garnet, Ruby

Past Life Memories
Amber, Amethyst, Aquamarine, Carnelian, Obsidian

Patience
Amber, Amethyst, Azurite, Tsavorite

Perception
Danburite, Epidote

Phobias
Aquamarine, Carnelian, Chrysoprase, Quartz

Physical Energy
Calcite, Carnelian, Herkimer Diamond, Garnet, Quartz, Spinel

Physical Strength
Bloodstone, Garnet, Diamond, Quartz

Physical Trauma
Bloodstone, Grossularite Garnet

Pituitary Gland
Moonstone, Rhodonite

PMS
Amethyst, Dolomite, Lapis, Magnesite, Rose Quartz

Positive Attitude
Aventurine, Hematite, Obsidian

Post-Surgical Healing
Bloodstone, Coal, Jet

Power
Aquamarine, Charoite, Red Jasper, Quartz, Tiger's Eye

Prophesy
Prehnite, Nebula Stone, Prasiolite

Prosperity Attraction
Aventurine, Amethyst, Aqua Aura, Bloodstone, Calcite, Citrine, Green Moss Agate, Garnet, Herkimer Diamond, Jade, Jasper, Malachite, Peridot, Salt, Spinel, Tiger's Eye, Tsavorite, Turquoise

Protection of Children
Blue Lace Agate, Green Moss Agate, Jade, Malachite Mother of Pearl, Ruby

Protection - General
Agate, Alum, Amber, Aventurine, Ammonite, Banded Agate, Beryl, Black Agate, Black Kyanite, Black Obsidian, Black Tourmaline, Calcite, Carnelian, Cat's Eye, Chalcedony, Chrysoprase, Citrine, Coral, Emerald, Topaz, Rock Salt, Topaz, Jade, Jasper, Jet, Labradorite, Lapis Lazuli, Lepidolite, Magnesite, Obsidian, Malachite, Moonstone, Ocean Jasper, Pearl, Peridot, Petrified Wood, Pink Kunzite, Prehnite, Pumice, Pyrite, Quartz, Quartz Crystal Clusters, Red

Jasper, Ruby, Rutilated Quartz, Sardonyx, Selenite, Serpentine, Smoky Quartz, Obsidian, Staurolite, Sulphur, Sunstone, Tiger's Eye, Topaz, Tourmaline

Protection - Angelic
Angelite, Selenite, Seraphanite

Protection During Astral Travel
Brecciated Jasper, Kyanite, Red Jasper, Yellow Jasper

Protection - Aura, Personal Energy Field
Fire Agate, Black Tourmaline, Labradorite, Sunstone, Tiger's Eye

Protection from Crime
Sardonyx

Protection from Disease/Illness
Chalcopyrite, Jade, Cavansite, Zircon

Protection from Evil
Agate, Beryl, Black Tourmaline, Blue Chalcedony Coral, Garnet, Herkimer Diamond, Malachite, Pyrite, Quartz, Salt, Sapphire, Turquoise

Protection from Evil Eye
Agate, Cat's Eye, Carnelian, Malachite, Topaz

Protection for Home and Other Buildings
Halite, Holey Stones, Salt, Riverstone, Quartz, Ruby

Protection from Theft
Ruby, Sardonyx, Zircon

Protection for Pregnancy and Childbirth
Ammonite, Geodes, Hematite, Lepidolite, Malachite, Moonstone, Picture Jasper, Rose Quartz

Protection Against Injury
Carnelian, Agate, Fluorite, Peridot, Smoky Quartz, Zircon, Turquoise

Protection Against Poison
Diamond, Serpentine

Protection from Psychic Energy
Amber, Amethyst, Angelite, Black Obsidian, Fluorite, Jade, Labradorite, Lapis Lazuli, Prehnite, Pyrite, Ruby

Protection - from Spirits
Black Sapphire, Chalcedony, Silkstone

Protection during Travel
Amethyst, Aquamarine, Chalcedony, Garnet, Herkimer Diamond, Jet, Malachite, Moonstone, Mother of Pearl, Tiger's Eye, Petalite, Jasper

Psychic Abilities and Increased Intuition
Amazonite, Amethyst, Apatite, Azurite, Botswana Agate, Cavansite, Celestite, Emerald, Fire Agate, Garnet, Green Calcite, Herkimer Diamonds, Holey Stones, Kyanite, Labradorite, Lapis, Meteorites, Moonstone, Opal, Orange Calcite, Quartz, Selenite, Super Seven, Tektite, Turquoise

Psychic Awareness
Amethyst, Kyanite, Lapis Lazuli, Copal

PTSD Easing of Symptoms
Lepidolite, Richterite

Public Speaking Fear
Celestite, Azurite, Blue Lace Agate

Purification
Calcite, Fluorite, Amber, Diamond, Lapis Lazuli
Halite, Salt

Radiation Exposure
Black Tourmaline

Rape Recovery
Calcite, Chrysocolla, Lapis, Black Tourmaline

Reconciliation
Calcite, Herkimer Diamond, Kunzite, Rose Quartz,
Rhodocrosite

Relationship Healing
Dalmatian, Diamond, Fluorite, Scolecite

Relaxation
Chevron Amethyst, Dalmatian Jasper, Jasper, King
Cobra Jasper, Red Jasper,
Richterite

Releasing Blockages
Ametrine, Bloodstone, Flourite, Malachite, Obisdian

Reliability
Garnet, Hematite Jasper

Relieving Burdens
Lodestone, Moonstone

Removing Obstacles
Kunzite, Quartz

Repressed Issues
Botswana Agate, Epidote, Peridot

Reproductive System
Garnet, Orange Calcite, Red Calcite, Garnet, Ruby, Moonstone
Responsibility Jasper, Bloodstone

Restless Leg Syndrome (RLS)
Chrysoprase, Lapis Lazuli

Rheumatoid Arthritis (RA)
Bloodstone, Garnet, Halite, Quartz

Romance
Almandine Garnets, Amber, Diamonds, Emerald, Pyrope Garnets, Red Coral, Red Garnet, Red Tourmaline, Rose Quartz, Ruby, Sardonyx

Schizophrenia
Celestial Quartz, Kunzite, Larimar, Lepidolite

Scrying
Obsidian, Quartz, Seer Quartz, Window Quartz

Self-Awareness / Self-Discovery
Chevron Amethyst, Labradorite, Quartz

Self-Confidence
Agate, Aragonite, Citrine, Dolomite, Garnet, Labradorite, Malachite, Moss Agate, Ruby, Sodalite, Tiger's Eye, Tiger Iron, Tourmaline, Turquoise

Self-Control
Black Obsidian, Dumortierite, Blue Quartz, Onyx, Sardonyx, Sodalite, Tiger Iron, Topaz

Self-Esteem
Amazonite, Carnelian, Copper, Kunzite, Rhodochrosite, Green Moss Agate

Self-Expression
Chysoprase, Howlite Garnet

Self-Acceptance
Aquamarine, Danburite, Opal Feldspar, Kunzite, Lepidolite, Rhodochrosite, Rhodonite, Rose Quartz, Ruby, Sodalite

Self-Realization
Aventurine, opal

Self-Reliance
Prasiolite Mother of Pearl

Selfishness to Decrease
Howlite, Ruby

Sexuality
Amber, Botswana Agate, Carnelian, Citrine, Diamond, Jade, Mexican Fire Opal, Red Calcite, Ruby, Rutilated Quartz

Serenity
Aquamarine, Blue Quartz (Dumortierite), Blue Tourmaline, Opal Emerald, Hawk's Eye (Blue Tiger's Eye), Jade, Jasper, Kunzite, Kyanite, Smoky Quartz, Tsavorite, Turquoise, Sapphire, Pink Kunzite

Shamanic Work
Iolite, Moqui, Moonstone, Obsidian, Yellow Calcite

Shielding
Amber, Black Tourmaline, Boji Stones, Hematite, Labradorite, Pietersite, Smoky Quartz Ruby

Sinusitis
Aventurine, Garnet Lapis Lazuli, Rhodochrosite, Smithsonite

Skin / Skin Disorders
Apophyllite, Amethyst, Aventurine, Azurite / Malachite, Blue Lace Agate, Botswana Agate, Carnelian, Chrysotile, Crazy Lace Agate, Dumortierite, Fancy Jasper, Garnet, Green Jasper, Moonstone, Moss Agate, Epidote, Mother of Pearl, Picture Jasper, Rainforest Jasper (Rhyolite), Spinel, Turquoise

Sleep
Jade, Lepidolite, Opal, Mica

Sleep Disorders
Amethyst, Aventurine, Hematite, Peridot, Moonstone

Sorrow
Apache Tears, Dolomite

Soothing
Rose Quartz, Blue Kyanite, Pink Kunzite

Spirit Contact
Jade, Prehnite, Tsavorite

Spiritual Development
Amethyst, Diamond, Citrine, Epidote, Green Onyx, Obsidian, Quartz, Selenite, Topaz

Spirituality
Amethyst, Calcite, Citrine, Clear Quartz, Hematite, Heliodor, Herkimer Diamond, Iolite, Lipidolite, Meteorites, Pearl, Rhodocrosite, Selnite, Silver Topaz, Sugilite, Turquoise

Spirit Guides -Contacting
Amethyst, Angelite, Apophyllite, Celestite, Herkimer Diamonds, Garnet Quartz, Selenite

Stability
Celestite, Chrysoprase, Citrine, Garnet, Hematite, Obsidian, Petrified Wood, Smoky Quartz, Tiger Iron

Stamina
Crazy Lace Agate, Dolomite, Sodalite, Spinel, Tiger Iron

Stomach Problems
Botswana Agate, Citrine, Peridot, Jasper, Obsidian

Strength
Agate, Carnelian, Citrine, Hematite, Herkimer Diamonds, Richterite, Tiger's Eye, Tiger Iron Rutilated Quartz

Stress
Aragonite, Azurite-Malachite, Bloodstone, Blue Kunzite, Brecciated Jasper, Calcite, Chevron Amethyst, Dolomite, Fluorite, Hematite, Kunzite, Labradorite, Lepidolite, Moonstone, Peridot, Picasso Marble, Richterite, Rose Quartz, Smoky Quartz,

Spinel, Staurolite, Sunstone, Turquoise

Success
Aventurine, Aqua Aura, Citrine, Green Moss Agate, Green Tourmaline

Success in Business
Aventurine, Bloodstone, Citrine, Chrysoprase, Garnet, Lepidolite, Leopard Skin Jasper, Malachite, Petrified Wood

Teaching
Glendonite, Lapis, Kyanite, Sodalite

Teeth and Gums
Agate, Amazonite, Aquamarine, Calcite, Dolomite, Fluorite, Howlite, Malachite, Spinel

Tension Headache
Amethyst, Blue Lace Agate, Cat's Eye Lapis Nevada.

Thinking
Dolomite, Fluorite, Hematite

Throat Bronchial and Lung
Amber, Ammonite, Angelite, Beryl, Bloodstone (throat infections), Blue Calcite, Blue Topaz, Chalcopyrite, Galena, Larimar, Malachite, Morganite, Opal, Tiger's Eye

Tissue Regeneration
Carnelian, Citrine, Garnet, Malachite, Turquoise

Thyroid Regulation
Blue Calcite, Rhodonite

Toxins
Amber, Amethyst, Botswana Agate, Citrine, Coal, Heliodor (Golden Beryl), Leopard Skin Jasper, Prasiolite, Tree Agate, Rutilated Quartz

Tranquility
Blue Lace Agate

Transition
Malachite, Obsidian, Green Tourmaline, Blue Sapphire

Transformation
Blue Kyanite, Bloodstone, Blue Sapphire, Charoite, Lepidolite, Malachite, Obsidian, Moqui Marbles

Trauma Healing
Diopside, Garnet

Travel by Water
Aquamarine

Travel in General
Amethyst, Aquamarine, Chalcedony, Garnet, Herkimer Diamond, Jet, Malachite, Tiger's Eye

Truth
Amethyst, Amazonite, Apophyllite, Blue Topaz, Celestite, Citrine, Emerald, Flourite, Garnet, Kyanite, Lapis, Selenite, Sodalite, Tiger's Eye

Tumor Shrinking and Prevention
Prasiolite

Ulcers
Chrysocolla, Peridot, Prasiolite

Unconditional Love
Kunzite, Rhodocrosite, Rhodonite, Rose Quartz

Vertigo
Cuprite, Malachite, Sapphire, Herkimer Diamond, Rose Quartz, Candle Quartz (Pine Apple Quartz), Angel Aura (Opal Aura), Aqua Aura, Lapis Lazuli, Morganite, Obsidian (clear), Quartz (clear), Red Jasper

Victimization
Calcite, Orange, Charoite, Chrysoprase, Garnet, Green Calcite, Hematite, Jade, Leopard Skin Jasper, Malachite, Orange Millennium™, Rose Quartz, Rutilated Quartz, Black Tourmaline

Vigor / Virility
Tiger Iron

Visualization
Iolite, Green Tourmaline, Holy Stones

Wealth
Fool's Gold

Weight Loss
Blue Peruvian Opal, Green Tourmaline, Heulandite, Moonstone, Rose Quartz, Spinel

Weight Gain
Unakite

Will Power
Alexandrite, Blue Tiger's Eye (Hawk's Eye), Garnet, Hematite, Red Jasper, Prasiolite, Sapphire, Tiger's Eye, Tiger Iron

Wisdom
Amethyst, Amber, Calcite, Celestine, Clear Quartz, Labradorite, Lapis, Malachite, Moonstone, Petrified Wood, Smoky Quartz, Snowflake Obsidian, Sodalite, Tree Agate

Wishes
Moonstone, Smoky Quartz

Worries
Petrified Wood

Wrinkles
Rose Quartz

Writing
Agate, Amazonite, Barite, Blue Topaz, Diopside, Fire Agate, Graphite, Kyanite, Lapis Lazuli, Sodalite, Variscite

Chapter 4 – Clean and Clear your Crystals

There are multiple methods for cleaning and preparing your crystals before use. The following are the basic methods to cleanse and prepare your new crystals before your first attempt to use them.

Cleansing with Water

Before using a crystal for healing or any vibrational purposes, they must be cleaned first. Crystals will have absorbed energy before you acquired them. This energy may not be conducive to your purposes. Crystals come from the earth, so when you buy or otherwise acquire one it may have dirt, fingerprints, or other matter on it. The first thing you need to do is to wash your crystal.

The best way to clean a crystal will depend on its type. Check the Mohs Scale of Mineral Hardness to make sure it is safe to clean it with water. If it is rated 5 or lower on the hardness scale it can actually dissolve in water and will need more delicate methods. Any crystal rated at least 6 can be safely cleaned with running water.

All of the precious and semi-precious gemstones such as diamonds, sapphires, emeralds etc. can be safely cleaned with water.

All of the crystals with names that end in "ite" are too soft to clean with water. These include Fluorite, Calcite, and any other "ite" Turquoise and Gypsum are also water-soluble crystals. Do not clean them with water.

Some Crystals are so low on the hardness scale that even brief exposure to water can start to dissolve them. When in doubt always check the hardness scale. You can also take a piece of steel and try to scratch a crystal. If it is soft enough to scratch it is too soft to clean it with a stream of water.

If you have bought, found, or otherwise acquired a crystal with mud on it, it more than likely has its growth matrix on. The matrix is the part of the earth that has grown the crystal. It is rich with mineral nutrients. Very carefully and gently remove the matrix with a small, soft, dry, brush such as you would use to clean jewelry. You can buy an inexpensive extra soft child's toothbrush for this. Clean slowly and carefully because it is possible that the crystal underneath is softer than the matrix that it has grown in.

If you are not having any luck removing the matrix with a brush, you can try soaking it in a bath of oxalic acid. Mix one-part oxalic acid into two parts water. Let it soak in this bath for a couple of days.

Once you have rid your crystal of its matrix, use a warm water bath and a medium stiff brush for coarse crystals, or a soft one such as a toddler's tooth brush for more brittle crystals. You can use a mild dish soap to help remove dirt. You can also pick out any dirt embedded in your crystal with a toothpick. Don't use metal objects to scrub your crystal or it may get scratched and damaged.

Another method to clean your crystal is to bathe it in water and sea salt. The addition of sea salt to the bath will add to the crystal's electrical vibrations. Be careful of this method with Pearls and Angelite which are too sensitive for using salt. Use any glass container for the bath and non-ionized sea salt. Never use a metal container. Use 1 or 2 tablespoons of sea salt per gallon of water. Soak the crystals for a day or 2 at the most. The water can come from a spring, a lake, a stream, or you can collect rain water for this purpose. It is best to avoid mineral water. Change the water after a day or so if it appears dirty. Do not dry your crystals but allow them to dry naturally in the sun or in moonlight.

Clearing your Crystal

Once the crystal is cleaned of dirt, it needs a spiritual cleansing or "clearing" to rid it of unwanted energy that it may have acquired so that these unwanted vibrations don't create obstacles for your intentions and the purposes for which you mean to use your crystal. You will also need to clear the crystals after each use. Crystals that are worn for jewelry should also be cleansed periodically since they pick up energy and you do not want to be wearing a crystal that has attracted negativity.

Clearing a crystal is a quicker process than cleaning them of physical dirt. If the crystals you are clearing is hard enough to use water on you can bathe them in salt water for up to 7 hours. However, if the crystals were used for a heavy exorcism, you may need to cleanse them for several days. Plastic containers are best for this. Glass containers can be used if you are careful not to drop the crystals in, since they may chip. Do not use metal containers. You only need use enough water to cover the crystals. The water should be about room temperature, never ice cold or hot. Spring water or ocean water is an excellent choice for clearing your crystals.

Another way to clear your crystals is to bury them. Crystals can be buried in a bowl of sea salt for cleansing. If using this method, you must be very careful not to let your crystals get scratched, because salt itself is also a crystal. Salt can also absorb moisture which could be a problem if using it to clear your crystal. If there is any dampness it can be soaked up by your crystal which could cause it to become dull in appearance. If you live in a humid climate where your salt has likely absorbed moisture it is best to avoid this method. Especially for crystals that are low on the hardness scale.

Another way to clear crystals of negative energy by burying is to place them back into the earth. Dig a small hole in a safe place and gently bury your crystal in it.

The safest way to use the burying method for clearing your crystals would be to bury them indoors. Using a small nonmetal container filled with potting soil or moss. Bury your crystal in the loosely packed soil or moss and leave it there for a few hours or even a couple of days. Extra care must be taken if you are burying a water-soluble crystal. If the potting soil or moss is the least bit damp you should set it out in the sun to dry first before using it. Feel free to use this soil afterwards for your garden or indoor plants. Having used it to clear your crystals will not have caused it any harm. Crystals can also be cleared by burying them in sand, but again there is the risk of scratching your softer crystals.

Another method to clear your crystals is by smudging. Just like herbs can be burned to clear a home of negativity they can be used in the same way to clean your crystals. You can burn incense, sage, cedar, lavender or sweetgrass, or even a combination of any or all of these. As they burn, take your crystals and pass them repeatedly through the smoke. Doing this for at least seven minutes will clear the crystal of any negativity. You can use a feather to fan the smoke over your crystals but do not use your hand or allow your hand to pass through the smoke or you may pick up the negative energy as it leaves the crystal. After clearing your crystal with smoke, it is a good idea to wash your hands in a purifying mix of salt water or to smudge yourself to clear away any negative energy that may have passed to you from the crystal. This is also good practice any time you have performed any healing ritual on anyone, in case their negative energy has passed to you.

Your own breath can be used to clean your crystals. Fist breathe deeply and slowly and picture in your mind all the negativity being blown away. Next pick up your crystal and imagine it as an extension of yourself. You and the crystal are one. Take a slow deep breath in through your nose and out through your mouth. As you slowly release your breath over the crystal imagine the negativity blowing away. Repeat this for several breaths,

Another method to clear your crystals is by channeling energy. First you must relax with several deep and slow breaths. Take your crystal in hand and imagine a flow of energy running through it. Picture a strong and powerful pure and positive energy passing through and being absorbed by your crystal. Picture a bright clean white light shining on and through your crystal.

Other Sources to Clear Your Crystals

Negative ions can clear your crystals. Electrical storms produce such ions. When lightening is expected to occur place your crystals outside. This can clear them of negative energy, however if your crystals are low on the hardness scale beware of leaving them out in the rain.

Negative ions are also generated from fire, for example burning a candle or the smoke of wood from a fireplace can cleanse your crystals. Do not place crystals directly into the fire as it can crack them.

Sunlight is also a source of positive energy that can clear your crystals. They can be placed out in direct sun, or even on your windowsill on a sunny day. The suns energy can be amplified by placing your crystals in a clear glass or bowl of water and setting it in the sunshine,

Moonlight is another source of positive energy for your crystals, the most powerful being that of the full moon. The best part about using moonlight to clear your crystals is that it is safe for all types so there is no need to worry about where they fall on the hardness scale or whether they are water soluble or not. On the night of a full moon, if you have a window that faces the moonlight set your crystals on the windowsill, or leave them outside in a safe place. Leave them to bask in the moonlight overnight but take them inside out of the sun during the day. Return them at night until the new moon begins.

Chapter 5 - Charging your Crystals

Equally important to clearing your crystal is charging your crystal. Clearing removes unwanted energy that poses obstacles to your intended purpose. Charging a crystal directs the energy towards your purpose and increases its abilities. It taps into the unused power that otherwise lies sleeping. In a way, charging your crystal is what wakes it up from its dormant state.

There are multiple methods for activating the power of your crystal.

Just as sunlight has the power to clear your crystal it also has the power to activate it. Sunlight is a source of ultraviolet rays which can charge your crystal.

Because crystals have been created in the earth and been nurtured by Yin energy (Female) It requires Yang energy (Male) as a source of renewal after being taken from the earth.

Light radiation from the sun can restore energy that has been drained from the crystal. How long it takes for the crystal to absorb this energy will depend on the type of crystal, how drained it is of energy and even the person who has been using the crystal and for what purpose it has been used.

A good starting point to charge and activate your crystal is 6 hours of sunlight one day a week. Some crystals will require more time to recharge depending on their type and for what purposes they have been used. The light radiation of the sun can charge your crystal for purposes of increased income, love, and vitality. After your crystal has spent it's 6 or so hours in the sun hold it in your hand and see how it feels to you. If you feel it is not charged enough you can always put it back into the sun the next day. Charging your crystal is like giving it a task to complete. You are giving it direction and purpose based on your intentions.

Try to be as specific as possible with your intentions and your crystals. For example, Love for a Pink Tourmaline, attracting intuition or psychic visions with an amethyst. Try to assign a specific purpose to your crystal and not bog it down with too many intentions.

Every crystal already has its own uniquely individual vibrational energies, but with use those energies can lessen or become depleted. Charging your crystal is like plugging in your phone when the battery dips below 50%. Your crystals need to be charged after use and after clearing them and before using them again for another purpose or whenever you get the feeling that their energy is weak.

Moonlight can be used to charge your crystals with positive energy. It is especially helpful for any of the whitish stones like quartz and opal.

Energy from the moon is helpful when you want to use your crystals for any mystical purpose or intent. To absorb this energy, place your crystals in the light of a full moon.

For other purposes such as attracting a new beginning you may want to set your crystals in the light of a waxing moon. For intentions such as lowering your debt or ridding yourself of an illness try setting them out in the light of a waning moon.

Passing your crystal through the smoke of incense that is instilled with the same intentions of the crystal can increase its energy. An example of this would be for instance using the smoke of Applewood incense which is associated with love to charge a crystal such as emerald which is also associated with love, thus increasing its positive energy to attract love. Also using crystals that are known to amplify power for instance Malachite can be charged with a power increasing incense like frankincense. You could also use an incense by its elemental association such as charging in the earth the crystals that are associated with earth.

There are also certain times in the planetary cycle and seasons that are associated with particular energies. For example, the autumn is associated with harvest and a good time to charge a crystal that you want to use to fulfill or harvest your desires. Spring Time is related to growth and new beginnings and a good time to charge a crystal with your intentions for attraction, or to bury in your garden to bring about an abundant growth. You can charge your yard or garden with the energy of crystals by burying them on your property. Burying near a pine tree is associated with healing, oak trees are associated with strength. To charge your crystals before burying on your property you can first bury them in flower petals or dried leaves, or first place it outside in a thunderstorm as previously discussed, the negative ions created by lightning will recharge its energy,

Another method of charging your crystals is with sounds. You can chant over your crystals or repeatedly ring a bell or chime in their presence. A tuning fork can be used to charge your crystals and so can music. Different instruments create various vibrations that are associated with different types of energy. The music you use to charge your crystals can be either live music or recorded. Another technique for charging your crystals is by using a pyramid. The shape of the pyramid can attract both spiritual and psychic energy, Pyramids when correctly made will create negative ions much like lightning. To use a pyramid for charging the crystal is placed under the frame and left for about 6 hours.

If your crystals are too large to fit under the frame, charge them by holding them above the top point of the pyramid, Imagine the energy of the pyramid and picture it in your mind coming out of the top point and into your crystal. Pyramids come in many different materials, including glass, metal, and even ones made of multiple different crystals.

Infusing It with Your Own Energy

You can infuse your crystal with your own energy by using mediation and visualization techniques. Just sit quietly with your crystal in your dominant hand and picture your own intentions and energy pouring into it, filling it up.

Chapter 6 - Activating Your Crystal

As previously discussed, charging your crystals provides them with energy, and activating them gives them direction in which to use that energy. Some crystals are considered to be sleeping until they are given the knowledge of their purpose.

Sleeping with a crystal under your pillow or holding it in your hands and rolling it back and forth you're your hands can help wake up its energy. Stating your intentions out loud along with positive affirmations can also activate your crystal. Visualize yourself protected by a white light and say so out loud. For example, "I am protected from harm by love and light"

Chapter 7 - Final Thoughts

Crystals are influenced by those who handle them, by the change of seasons and amount of light passing through them. Crystals have their own energy but absorb the energy of other sources. The energy a crystal has will be influences by the mineral it formed from, it's location in the earth the length of time over which it formed and the elements in which it has been surrounded.

When light travels through a crystal it meets the crystals own energy. The way in which this energy reacts can transform or amplify that energy.

After you have used a crystal for any intent or purpose the crystal has picked up that energy which is why it is important to remember they need to be cleansed of that energy before using them again. If a crystal had been left alone away from any outside influence and not used for an extended amount of time it would over time cleanse and recharge itself, but for practical reasons that is not a preferred method since you likely don't want to wait that long to use it again.

After cleaning and recharging and activating your crystal you can perform a dedication when you are ready to use your crystal. Sit somewhere quiet where you can be undisturbed. Hold your crystal in your hands and take slow deep breaths with your eyes closed. Think of the purpose for which you want to use your crystal and repeat it to yourself three times. Picture these intentions filling your crystal.

You could also write your intention 3 times on a piece of paper and set your crystal on top of the paper where it will absorb your intentions. If your intentions are not for yourself but to help someone else you can also place your crystal on top of a picture of that person.

Another technique to program your crystal with your intentions is with your breath, Hold the crystal in your hand and concentrate on your intention while releasing short breaths onto your crystal. Turn the crystal in your hands and release a breath onto each side.

Alternatively, you can breathe deeply and slowly while holding the crystal, breathing out your energy and inhaling energy from the crystal while concentrating on your intentions. Always use your crystal with positive intentions. Never breathe bad intentions or negative thoughts into your crystal. Always use crystals for the greater good.

When not in use your crystals can be kept in a cloth pouch or silk bag, storing it this way protects it from absorbing any unwanted negativity and also from scratches or other physical harm. Don't forget to clean and recharge it after each use.

I hope this book has been a helpful start to guide you on the many possible uses of crystals, and that it will inspire you to learn more about all the positive ways crystals can be used.

If you enjoyed this book and found it helpful in learning about Crystals, I would be forever grateful if you could leave a review on Amazon. Reviews are the best way to help your fellow Crystal healers find the helpful books.

If you're interested in learning about Tarot Card Reading, make sure to check out my book 'Tarot Reading for Beginners'.

www.ingramcontent.com/pod-product-compliance
Lightning Source LLC
Chambersburg PA
CBHW042233090526
44588CB00001B/5